Stars Drink Milky Language

Stars Drink Milky Language

Songs for Infinite Love

&

Eternal Mystery

Stars Drink Milky Language ~ Copyright © 2010–2011 C. J. Donegan.
All rights reserved. No part of this work may be used or reproduced in any manner whatsoever without written permission from the author except in the case of brief quotations in critical articles or reviews. For information please contact the author at:

The Sacred Grove Foundation: sacred.grove.foundation@gmail.com

The beautiful galactic imagery was captured by the Hubble Telescope. Please thank Whomever you wish for this. Such beauty remains untold, undiscovered even.

All images used in this book are the exclusive property of the contributing artists: Matthieu Aubry, Christina Carney, Ludmila Disa and Nickole Alexandria Pepera. All images are generously shared for use in this book alone—permission for any further use for any purpose must be obtained by contacting the artist of each work. A limited amount of prints & more imagery may also be available from each artist. And to the four of you, you do have my heartfelt gratitude for entrusting your work to me.

This mandala is offered by Charles Gilchrist on the website bearing his name. Thank you for sharing this sacred geometry for the world to see

The moon appeared in her fullness
when women took their place
around the altar

~ Sappho

Contents

One: Life, Initiation and Descent

Incantation 12

Two Islands 13

Smoke Rises Curling 15

I saw the darkness 17

Know 19

You Picked a Flower for Me 23

If 26

The Abyss 27

Standing Solid 29

In the Chaos 31

the mirror to itself one day 35

Across the Floor 36

Egg of Mystery 39

But When it Rains 44

Lost Seeds 48

Two: Death, Darkness and the Dreaming

Ereshkigal 51

Milky Night 52

Mandalavision 57

Enkidu 59

Nothing.. 74

Three: Rebirth and InfinEternity

Drink from the Heart.. 76
Your Heart... 78
You are the Message... 80
Ultraviolet... 87
Like the Moon... 88
The Path.. 89
The Leaves...91
Circle of Water..93
True... 95
All is Love.. 98

Afterword.. 101
Appendix I: The Images 103
Appendix II: The Artists 105
Dream On... 108

Table of Consciousness

1.

Illuminated and Beloved
Creator of All

we thank you

may we learn to offer our eternal love for the infinite blessings of life—

such beauty to us remains

unseen

undiscovered

Infinite

May we live and die by these words

May I breathe in this vision when the oxygen is gone

May we drink in deep from your Love when our well is dry

When my heart overflows from too much spinning
love flies forth to all the corners of the world in song

Come back forgotten lover

Come back to the beloved Source from which your life water flows

Incantation

Poesis
Incantation

Sow the seeds of magic
The mystic tree grows in
The poetic field—

Imagination
Eleusis

In the city of gnosis
Will I live my life
At the river of love
Bathe my tired body

In the rich black midnight soil of poetry
Will the silky stalk rise again
And greet the crescent Moon

Two Islands

                          To swim between two islands

An island of the sun

                    the land of the warrior

                                                glimpse the truth

                      seize the moment

                         run

                      free the slaves

One island beneath a crescent moon

                      fresh salubrious breezes

                                              enchanting melodies

                  a mystic softly singing

Please, lower the Veil
slowly
don't burn the vision

And through the dark water

Down where the roots of the islands

grow in a river of luminescent fire

the host of whales swims calling to the dreamers—awaken

Awaken to the invisible orchestrations of life

Smoke Rises Curling

The smoke rises
curling through the grass

Dawn is a thousand love songs of
bluegreen
rose and silver

Life
fragile flower
guarded by time
and by death

the shell of my heart cracked open from so much pain

collective memory
huddled weeping mountains of souls
bloodrape and cinders
flying through the air
on the path to their release

There is no end to all this loving

I saw the darkness

I saw the darkness,
the evil and
the fear

and inhaled,
holding the end of its song
within me for
moments of
tension
and transformation.

There is a lightness
an effervescence
a release into a crystal song.

Fear dances with Love
and fear is transformed
melted in the sacred
Fire

I send this out through my guts

my chest

my arms fingers and soul

into the tip of the sword

that dances in the air.

Know

This is what I know

This truth cannot be repressed any longer

This truth flies forth

Enlightenment is now—*loving you in the coiled garden a barefoot dream*

And has always been

It is now

Awaken

open your heart

to Love

Now feel me warm

flutter wings

butterfly eyes

breath color

birth breathe

Let us walk out on the beach beneath the stars

Let me hold you in the tender place

In the touch of heart to heart

This is what I know

You turn me over

My head is down in the earth

My feet have wings

My sand runs out and I am empty again

I think of you and I am full of air and winged flight

I am sick like a moth in champagne

From the first time that I gazed upon your soft glow

I have felt a burning knife of unseen love in my heart of hearts

It turns slowly and pleasure floats upwards

It stops turning and pain runs in the depths

Someone whispers in my ear

I walk around in the night

The mist moves around me

Is this night my truest friend

The ways this feeling grows and blooms

It blooms within me

and reaches upwards to a central sun

that is the hope of your heart

at once opening within our naked embrace

I look into the color of your eyes in the sunlight
I want to dance, a bumblebee in your sunflower field
I want to disrobe your caution with my heart and stand naked before All,
together with you in humble divinity

I look at the Moon and I think of you
I walk around at night
I am drunk—*in you my galactic core melting in mandalas a planet of love*
In you feel strange walk naked in wet fields
Amongst the soft dewy plants as we dream together living alone with all

I have known you forever friend, immortal mythos
I know you
I have known these things
In this life I gazed upon you and recognized you
This is frightening, this truth

This I know
I have tried to avoid this magnetic truth
I have tried to count the ways that this could not be true

I am a fool, afraid to walk up to you and bow down low

I am afraid to hand you the sword and bare my breast

I want to lead you by the hand into the fields of stars

I want to gaze deeply into the mirrored lake of numinous consciousness

Breathe deeply—*a world of love your eyes inside my secret dream*

This is love

This is Samadhi unfolding in a reversal of time

This is love

This is all I know

You Picked a Flower for Me

Death

a voice said
the great gaping maw

Death—your death
your own death
Is your greatest witness

May it see your greatest moments
when perhaps you suspect
its eternal gaze
as eyes of stone
see an equinoctial aurora
and the solstice moon

one thousand years pass before one day my love

Find the path within
and run lungs full of life
Run
to the mountain that is beyond the maze

I wore a tragicomic mask
my face splitting open
Up and
upwards from within

we walk along the edge of the river

Spring is opening itself to the world
its blossoms reach forth in their living sacrifice

I try to crystallize every moment together
seeing even now its eternal expanse
the ever present now as it leaps forward
and falls into the descending trough of the wave
to disappear, seemingly forever.

You picked a flower for me
along the edge of the water.
Its long face spoke vegetal wisdom for days
as it leaned forward over the glass.

Even now,

thinking back

at everything I wonder if I've lost

the moment – gone forever –

a chance.

It had to have been then.

The flower,

slowly dying,

cut from the vine

Its face burned into my memory

even now.

As I look up at the distant stars and wonder

this moment feels alive—*blood moon beaches*

years ago years without number

The warm air pregnant with meaning

The cool flow of the wind

Clouds dance in slow progression

I kiss you

You cut me

We are born

If

If the world feels cold

the soul sucked out

and broken

eyes red dry from crying

you can not weep

A cataclysm, the loss of soul

Shadow drunk

Return to me in the fresh freedom beyond this

and we will turn the earth over

Pull together grassy dreams

and take to the wind

The Abyss

Look deep into the abyss that swallows time

How could something this abstract be so much more visceral
more terrifying than being within five paces of a running bear—*Alive*

There is no fear in
hitchhiking—
the vast and cold desert
the unknown
the starry rivers;
or in the
Knife attack—
steel rapes the wind
the traveler ducks
and skips away

There is no fear in
adrenalin
run
the night is old
the air is young

There is no fear in the abyss
only dark magnetic potentiality
We dream in worlds of unknown sex
Spiraling river 'neath the skin of reality

There is no fear in death—

There is only fear in the long descent

In the forgetting of origins

Do not ever forget, o spinning lovers
To return to your galactic sun

She has written her Secret Names upon my heart
A singing vine revealed a divine library of souls

All-Colors bled freely into
a supernova of unseen dreaming

Standing Solid

I do not want

Your admiration

Loathing

Lust

Or envy

My dear talented poetic girl—

I only want to discover you

Revealing the Mysteries

Hidden

Unknown.

I do not want to write a beautiful poem for you.

I only want to live through the nights of stone

Death

Alone.

I do not want you to be my friend—

Only want you to be a woman

Standing solid on the Earth

Unafraid to love me
Through the nightmarish
Inchoate madness of life.

In the Chaos

Individuation is cooking in the fires of self and crisis

When we integrate extreme pain

trauma or challenging circumstances,

we may notice
that deep in the chaos

is an ocean of life

beauty

and music.

the mirror to itself one day

i fear at times that you do not see
but your own projected dreams of me

egotism and vanity can only mask
insecurity and wounding for so long

the perfect polished plate—a negative state
the past all around then—shattered like glass

wake up and live the life you have been dreaming

dream the life you have been struggling to wake up to

Across the Floor

I love the way

she slides

unchained daimonic child

in fertile waves of flaxen dream

dark matter inside

the foaming mouth of ocean's tide

at the end of time we dance in flames—

she turns the key

an opening

a breath

undeath forever we live in

a hidden nautilus of our love

a shell my eyes

my eyes untied

like kite strings streaming

Flowers never dry when they are dreaming

I love the way she turns my eye

No shooting star—this falling sun

would burn the earth with her desire

The virgin huntress

at the feast

her unborn king

She leads me out into the forest before dawn to see

The silver crowning of the ancient Moon

I love her way

This dearest one I do
I love her
And this is not all

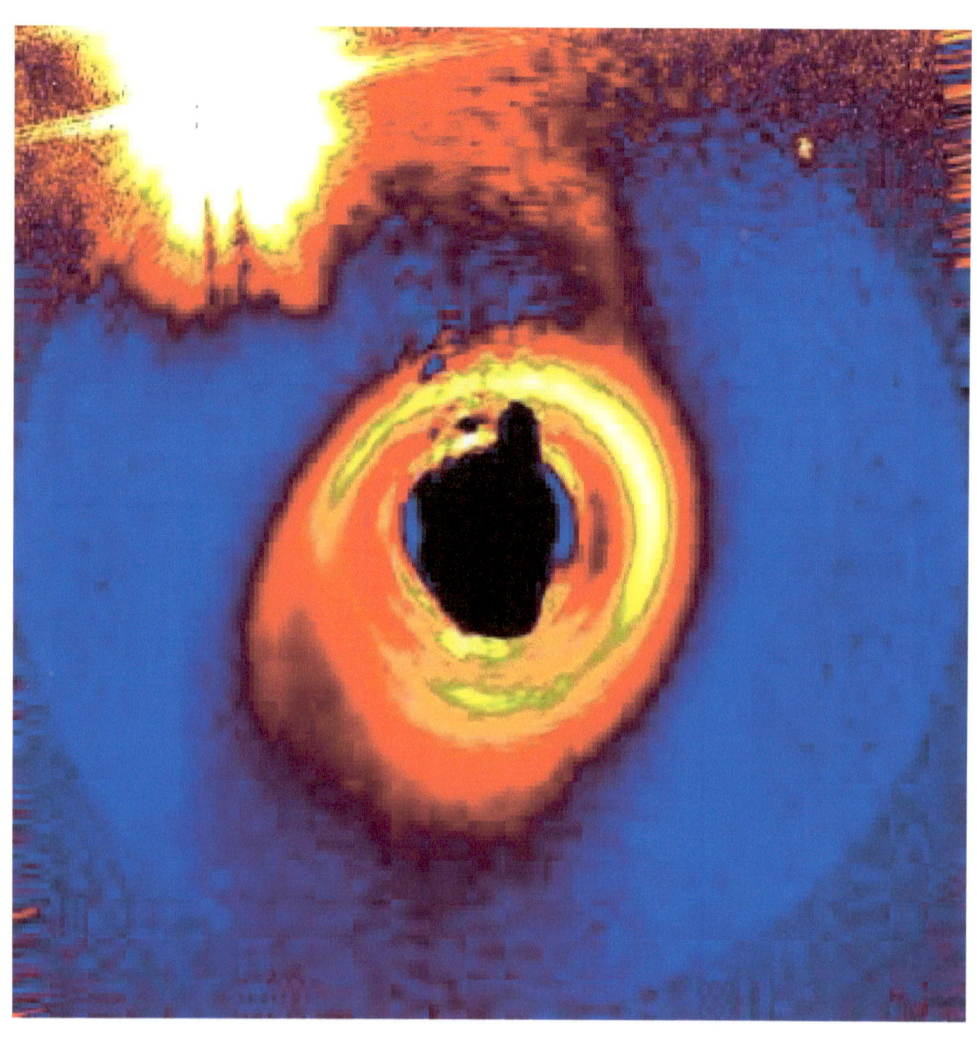

Egg of Mystery

If she had not washed my eyes
with minstrel blood
then I would still be blind.

I've known you forever,
Yet still, a mystery to me

We had wandered in the cave for days, our lights burnt out—
The walls were cold stone prisons
These nightmarish visions consumed our essence
Like invisible parasites sucking on luminous bones

Damp and cold and afraid

No soul-fires burned in these cavernous depths
This night seemed endless cold like stone,
heavy as the echo of your own tomb—

Doorways dreamt we dreaming in the cave
Doors windows chambers fires crackling
Casement breeze smells seasons' fresh messages

We dreamt doorways in the stone

Passages to sunlit halls seawind cliffs

freedom to create

to create the moon and shine

Then, after darkness and time had melded

into an unconscious throbbing flow

you awakened us in this endless night

You found me sleeping on the clay floor—

an egg of mystery unto myself

You broke me open and put me in

Your new burning flame

Breathe inside my vulvic heart Lady Life

Kiss me deep, I breathe inside your earthen sighs

You taste like milk—

My feral tigress

black-violet ribbons of light that is not seen

I've known you forever,

Yet still, a mystery to me

I slip into you like the sea

I love you like life

I love you like life when the hot sword enters the heart

Cling to me in the night and open

Flowers open to the cool and unseen mysteries before the Dawn

Drink the milky nectar

But When It Rains

Your silent vanishing

to me
conspires to efface
the moon and stars
for all their glory.

All my screams are muted—
blood boiling
heart choking
and tears invisible

but when it rains.

Since you disappeared
all of my pens are rusty
and full of sand.

I am left with only nails
hammers
and the silence
of

living

breathing

trees

Lost Seeds

I reach down
into the dark
small space

fingertips feeling for
the lost seeds
and am penetrated in a moment—

A long thin needle
is halfway
through my finger

horizontally stretching
on both sides
shining

I cannot feel a bit of pain
but excitement
fear and fascination

when you put your
invisible embrace in
kissed
straight through
the arrow

I slowly pull
the needle out
shining silver as you

move in the night air—
no longer does this
kiss right through

Ereshkigal

Ereshkigal

darkest

sister **dream**

ultraviolet serpent-hair
darkest matter
blackest eyes of night
yin magnetic
Ereshkigal

infinite possibility

stardrunk light

open your cool mouth

to me

Milky Night

I sense a new smell upon your lips,

Death my waiting bride.

Is it the fragrant cedar

In your smiling earthen sigh,

as you wait patiently for me to die

Come play with me in the Milky Night

You say

And we shall dance in silver ocean spray

Dark matter

Stardream

Smell the wind

My blood my breath my sex, this pull-

Such longing to return, like the tide

Lagrimas

Your fertile cave is cool mossy warm

with unformed longing to be born.

II.

Death my Angel
oldest Friend
Queen of Leaves

How your whispers sound like breeze

Scatter ashes to the winds

Feed the loam
this sweet release

Symbolic
Source
Golden
Fleece

Oblivion is easy
When you just fall like leaves

I never missed you in our sleep; forgotten home-

Your hair is soft as maize silk, even vegetal

And yet unseen like songs unsung

Till silky coiling threads reanimate the bone

III.

The cool silver disk

Plays gazing in its sky life

Water crystals sleep

Mandalavision

I close mine eyes to see
the shimmering play
of rainbow energy

An archetypal flux forms
the dance
Unending crystalline geometry
enchants

Dark lady iris
beyond all time
a new wine kiss—your vine, this bliss

An archetypal flux forms
The dance
That crystalline geometry
enchants

Enkidu

Dear friend
Where did you go

O Enkidu now departed
Wild man of the Ancient Forests?

How the women must have torn their hair
Clawed their breasts
In our city by the River
I did not have the courage to go back and see them place you
In the Boat of Heaven
Let the River take him

I wandered in the Wilderness
Lost to all but the Moon and the singing Trees

Why have you left me—
King of a mound of shit,
All good things now departed,
Come the Flood to wash the sins of men

This I know, you sacrificed yourself so that I could linger

When the Angel of Death came singing to collect
This harvest; cultivated lunatics and bloodflowers
The bluest gardens of twilight—
To swim drunk
In a sunken city of nightclouds
I run down to the Sea

II.

I fell down maddened, by the sea,
Barefeet, lips cracked, naked dream
For days not food could touch my tongue,
The Ocean mist told me stories of the Way
A sexy-sorrowful feathered spray
Timeless in her laughter;
Fucking back encroaching Death for a thousand Nights
To birth the Day
Even if it is the one last time

Give us just one more hour,
Great Goddess of the misty mounds
A sensuous slide—the massive beloved beast
She rides the Earth in sacred copulation
To entice the timeless Sun,
Rise, as if for the last ride in the East

She slays me with the Sword of Truth
So that I could know and be born
I wash the blade in the Ocean
She slays me with the Sword of Beauty
So that I may suffer and sing.
I wash her blade in the Ocean

And blow the horn across the azure leagues
This spiraled shell gives birth to sound
To mark the falling of the holy Trees

III.

Why did we transgress
The bounds of the Sacred Forest
Why pass the limits of the Goddess with
Profane emboldened steps

You wandered as innocent
The ancestral boughs near the edge of the Forest,
Its beasts and berries so kindly opening

Why did I bring you in my quest
A new religion we would be
Kings, heroes, new gods

Why have I defiled my city,
Oppressed my people,
And carved you in my form

Why did we transgress
The bounds of the Sacred Forest
Why pass the limits of the Goddess with our
Profane emboldened steps?

One of these two men must die,
To pay the bloodprice of the Celestial Bull
When I paused, heart-in-throat
You stepped forward at the dreamcliffs of Death—

I will go to the primordial Waters
I will swim in the deepest blue
The Abzu that replenishes the archaic flesh
in liquid primacy

I drove my chariot in the rain
Sky-bolts silhouetting the arms of Trees
Maddened horses, the long slow slide
I ended sideways in the River
Climbing up and out with not a scratch

I said *Be careful out there man—you never know.*
And the very next day

Why say anything at all

IV.

Nobody knew the way you loved that form of steel and glass
You were both 42 years old
When you flew through its fragile shell
Breaking the bonds of this world

This River
This city
This seed

Renewal from the Abzu
Passing through the underworld
Recreation in the fires
And cooling
The primordial depths of the Water
Abzu

Forget the Forest
Forget the creatures at Dawn
Forget the burning light of the Sun
Forget the midnight copulations in littoral breeze

Softly now She is singing:

We come to you

From across the Sea

Only one can go

Who will it be

V.

This is it,

Ziusudra said,

The secret of the righteous ones

What hidden truths they did not know

A singing flower told them so

This is it

Let the Moon rise forever

Let the Moon rise one time

and always

There is no time

There is no illusion

There is only the Moon

Dying, reborn

Forever

In passage through the underworld

And the primordial ocean, Tiamat,

The Abzu,

And then in ascent to the highest celestial

Paradise

She whispers in every Oceanic cell

And Earth-born current,

This is the Way

This is the eternal One

Dancing along this path with your Water

I tug and pull you upwards

To the knowledge of the spheres

Of the spinning

Of the flight forever through the Stars

And it went on, so beautifully this song

Melody remembered innocence

Before the breast was lost

This song, well sung I awaken

From the madness of my quest
From heroism
I awakened for the first time

I then felt the weight of it, and
Bathed in the waters of this arcane Rose
For the very first time the innocence returns
Washing the blood-weight in the knowledge of milk

I close my eyes

A snake smelt the fragrance of the plant and ingested its sacred budding form

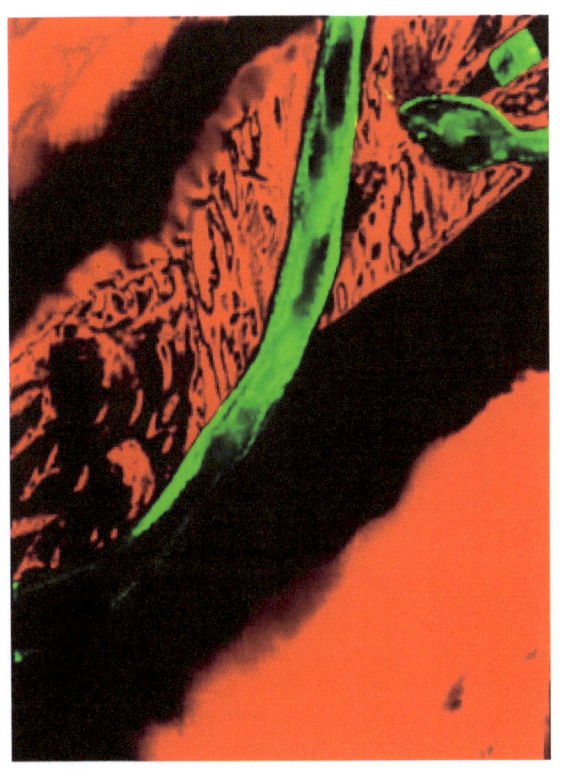

*It shed its skin
and stealthily crept away*

O the holy Water
Fall the tears

Drown my eyes
In all that's been

The great years
Born from below

Seeping upwards from the depths, in
The eternal renewal

Rise to the highest
To fall slowly on the Mountains,
Softest snow

Now gone into the depths,
Immortality's fading Flower,
I walk silently into the West
    Then to Death—

To the rebirth of the
Waters

And unknown formless
swimming

Nothing

I have nothing
and in this nothingness
is the seed of
everything that is
and ever will be

I have no one
and here in naked solitude
I am flowing outwards into everyone and
everything
at moments of disintegration
implosion
and nebular creation

I dissolve as one
into this
timeless loving of You.

You are creation's
flowering fountain—
orchid lava

cooling in the oceans

of our tears

                    You are the mist rising over the fields at dawn

Drink from the Heart

Réaltaí Deoch ó mo Chroí

Tonight my heart implodes into a billion suns
You birds, psycheins and unspoken dreamlike glances—you who knew me best
of all—come to my aid when my body falls into the worming mass
I am unbroken yet eternally shattered like glass
The blood colors I always loved the best—ultraviolet breathes the crimson moon
in its dancing rebellion against our paltry order

Take me out of your breast, my dove, and plant me deeply in the
desert of the Veils
There we will thirst and we shall find the deep hidden water
An infinite garden of soft verdant subtlety
Silky knots of luminous mystery
Unwound into endless rivers of moonlight
True copulations are forever unseen,

Flowerlove is the dream of long starry sleep

The milky tongue and the honey breast you may keep

You cut me open, Beloved

You slay me from within my own resurrection

Stars drink from the heart
Stars drink milky language
Stars drink from my heart
But you, Beloved, for you they may only sing

Your Heart is a Rose

Your heart is a rose
that would wish to open
only in the cool mists
before dawn

But you must protect it and nurture it

You must be the secret garden
in which it can safely open
and share its sweet nectar
with the world

You are the Message

Love—

All is love

We are the dancing steps of Love in the Gardens of Eternity

This world, this universe, every muscular fiber, neural pathway, even each drop of water and blood in our bodies—all the elements are notes in the greatest orchestral vibration—a song of creation

The universe is a neverending musical gift composed for the Beloved

We rise we dance we explode and then descend, falling like embers in the high summer air

We disintegrate into the loam, and in the chaotic webs of nebular creation we are born again; fresh, smooth as a river stone, unbroken—

immersed in the ancient galactic memory of all of the beauty, the ecstasy and traumatic pain that has ever been

This is the way of our life

This is the ocean of love in which we live

But how could one make such abstract, seemingly illogical claims

How could one even know such a thing

I know because this is our song

Please do join in the music, austere lover and forgotten son

This is the time of your discovery; the unknown music of love awaits—

I am love

We are love

All is love

I read the words that were written in my own heart before I knew of linear time

I am a cool, blue burning oasis in the desert of nothingness

I hear whisperings of the cosmic serpent, like a warm wind tickling my inner ear

I am one with the breath that is breathing me into existence

Between the moments I would disappear, but for the breath of the Beloved, lighting the lamp of my soul

I cry tears of joy that clean the wounds carved with an invisible sword

I am alive in my own death

I am the pomegranate ripening on the World Tree

And in this vessel, this bottle floating in the infinite seas, you are the message within my sealed container

You are the poem of twilight winds

You are the voice calling to me from across the shore

The flower opens within us

Its sweet milky fragrance releases perfumed knowledge before the dawn

Beloved Queen of the Aurora, your signs are all around us

I water your roots with tears of joyous pain, made holy by where they have fallen

Come to me before the night ends

I die in you and am reborn

As do the singing whales, every bird, the holy trees, even every single blade of grass I call your name in devotion

You are the One in which I melt,

like the crimson sun dipping into the waiting sea

My fragile heart turns to ash and takes flight on the western wind when You inhale

You pull me back inside

Your Heart is the womb in which I incubate; the umbilicus overflows within my chest

I would sing, but only with your hidden words can my mouth take shape

You are creation folded within itself—the portal to infinity that is within nothingness

Both within and without, you defy your own law, the logic of causality, of past-present-future

You are all places within one moment, within one pomegranate seed

You are the diamond star from which the forms have emanated forth

You humble yourself on every plane—abundance is your mystery

How could I say what dreams of you I have treasured in

7 years beneath the Earth

Your essence moves me, reaching within to unlock the magic door

You are the knowing key to my own cage, an illusory prison fashioned by our previous and unconscious assumptions

I am the bird that flies to you at dusk, when the sweet honeysuckle
ignites the torches of the senses
You are my land of milk and honey; undying in warm caves of
radiant and ultraviolet darkness

What am I that is not in you
I see you in every face
I watch for you through the casement of solitude
You are everything, yet never cease to be formlessness itself
I cannot see you, but listening, I hear your ancient song
enchanting the drumbeat of my heart

You are my Queen and I am your fool
Give me the wine of your own lips
I am already intoxicated with your water and your words

You shelter falcons in my heart
I make the long journey for your promise of water
The depths of space are cold
Yet from the wounded perspective, we see your raiment of stars
The desert is a burning wasteland of initiation
You are the flower that waters itself when there is no rain
Would I drink just one time from your sweet language of milk
I feel ready enough to die when you call me home
Yet strong within me is the fire of your life

I am your slave, composing the footsteps of the hidden way to beauty

In the Castle of Nothingness I await your audience
Reveal to me the secrets of your ecstatic pain
Unveil yourself so slowly, just one layer in
a thousand years, my mystic rose
The thorns are delicate joy, while the inner fragrance is the
unsung secret, the love from which the numberless galaxies were born
And here I am, gazing out the long hours at your green valleys, nearly
annihilated by the potency of the wind and the singing of the trees
I wish to see the ocean within
You are my deep water
I wonder that there is no knowing, there are no words for what we feel when you
are stretching out my growing boughs, when you are twisting me in
the fire of your hermetic forge
I beg of you—unchain me from myself
Take me into your breast and hold back the hunters of the doe
Turn me into the forest king to be devoured by your blessed lupine lips

We are born, we live, we die
For my death I want the orgiastic pleasure of the hungry lioness
But for eternity I want only you
There is never enough dew until we find you in the eyes of the assassin
Now all is dancing silver moonlight, immaculate and unborn
This is the union that creates the new wine

I am the grape that breaks open beneath your holy feet
You are the wine that bubbles forth from my stone heart
I am the living sacrifice that you place upon the altar of
your own inner sanctum
Make me the bow that slides into the untouched strings of
your deepest hidden instrument
You are the music that I follow, lost in the maze of my own nothingness
There is no other way
Riding on your own luminescent dragons we take the river of life
into the night of death
You are the mouth that opens to me
Take me within your secret heart
Light the fires again
We are the burning orchids at the end of time
Our many petals are soft, resplendent with the kisses of paradise
We are dancing in the fire that does not consume

I am your humblest of messenger-fools; you are the Message
The message is Love
All is love
Love is all

Let your children see the universe—whole and beautiful
May You be blessed now and forevermore

Ultraviolet

Burn

Burn with a cool blue flame

Slow

Solemn

Silently singing the ancient Name

Like the Moon

All is Love

At the beginning and in the end
the Universe is composed of angelic music

Like the moon I am a soft blue reflection of You
a ripple spreading outwards
at the speed of sound

The Path

I think of how many billion years have passed

while Earth melded herself into a body

out of the flying chaos and unformed being of the Cosmos

until finally after billions

millions more revolutions around the Sun

She cooled her primal flow in the cold solitude of space

and aeons of tempestuous romantic rains

And in these ineffable billions of years

slowly does life crawl forward—

Archaea, Amborella, ferny forests of humid, untold stories—

until after these solitary and infinitely hungry ages

you are formed like Earth out of chaos untold

How precious to me

each small, rich moment with you

How acutely painful is your disappearance

I will be fine—pain is an ancient, mute shadow now turned ally by necessity

I knew this day would come

ever since

We breathed ourselves into being, into life

But you—what will you do now with all of this which you are

You are the love song of the aeons

Your precious heart and complex body is

the artistry of the Universe

What will you do now in this precious moment

What do you do with all this love

The Leaves

The leaves

the leaves

Look to the leaves

I see us together in a circle of dreams.

We stumble and rise

We laugh and we cry;

You carry me on when I fall by your side

The circle is ancient,

though not a day old-

woven in vines

eternal the tide.

The leaves,

the leaves –

always look to the leaves

when time bids you forget

the long dreams of trees.

Circle of Water

Standing in the center

Of a circle of Water

For ever—to tell you only this—

I *love you* ∞

Always

Eternity bows to Infinity—*breath of nights invention unknown colors stardream*

Love at first sight is deep recognition; the portal opens when you step through

How perfect this circle is then—

me at the center

one day

and you at the rim

You the next time

At the center will be

Forever loving me

                                     there is no line in time

                                       forever only this Moment

                                       is forever this Moment is

                                     welcome again to the Infinite Now

                                     walk inside this secret garden

                                                      open arms

                                     as you step through to me

                     inside the center of this liquid sphere our love

                            Miraculous Mystery of the ages

This love is like water

Drink deep from my loving cup

This fountain flows never ending

True

True Love does not need anything in return

Love gives freely to drink from its overflowing cup

True Love is like Water

That the thirsty pilgrims drink in the burning wastelands of the soul

True Love is not some crazy, head-over-heels infatuation

True Love is grounded in the deep soils of the Numinous Source

True Love is Freedom

And Freedom is truly Love

There is no other reality besides Love and the reality of Soul

All else is but a dream—

Awaken to the mysteries of the heart

Free your soul to fly in the

Hummingbird fields of nectar-vision

There are deeper colors here that exist beyond the senses

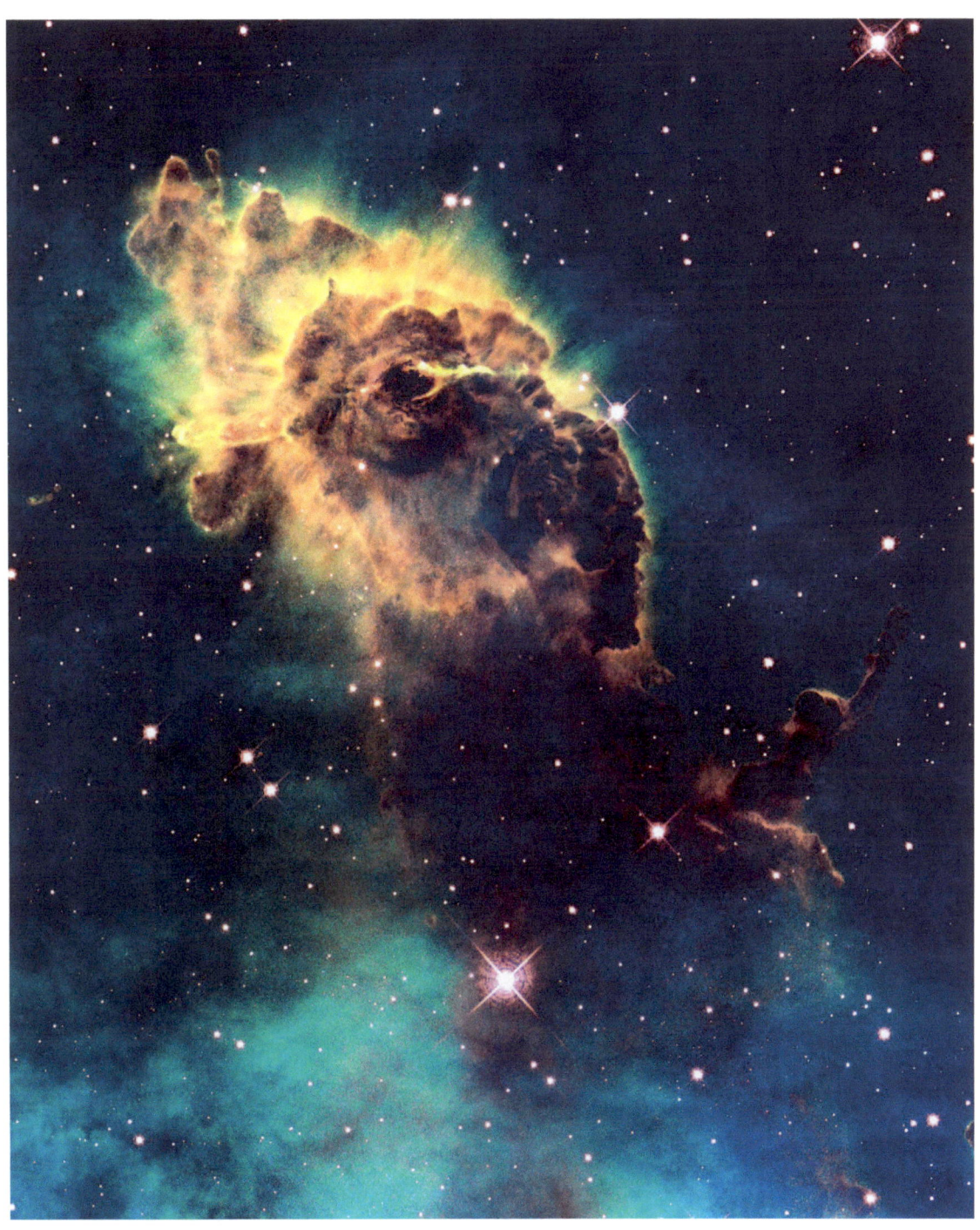

All is Love

At the beginning and in the end
The Universe is composed of angelic music

Like the Moon
I am this soft blue reflection of You,
ripple spreading outwards
at the speed of sound

Awakening

awakening

An Infinite Mystery of Love Unbound

You are an Infinite Mystery awakening to Love

Pillar and Jets HH 901/902 — Hubble Space Telescope ▪ WFC3/UVIS

NASA, ESA, and M. Livio and the Hubble 20th Anniversary Team (STScI) — STScI-PRC10-13a

All of these miraculous deep space images were captured by the Hubble Telescope and the Hubble Team. Images are displayed namelessly in this book so that we can discover them freely. These same visions & more are offered to the world at:
http://www.hubblesite.org/gallery/

~ Many heartfelt thanks to the entire Hubble Team. May We All continue to support open exploration of the Unknown and Peaceful Ventures into Space for the Future of our World

Afterword

Poetry to me is life itself.
I write to discover you—
To love you more deeply and
Sweet
I write to live
I write to be alive in a way mysteriously more
Real
I write to dream the Dream
I write to discover the beauty that was lost.
I write to celebrate the sacred beauty that is
Now.

Poetry can chart the course, leading the soul through the dangers and pains of life.

In the time period that these poetic works have gestated and been born, I have been living through some turbulent events. And now that we as people have faced everything from heartbreak to the loss of loved ones, to murder, genocide and environmental tragedies, it seems to me now more important to flourish, to express, to love and to sing. Ah, life. You fragile flower. Open to us now your sweetest nectar.

If we do not open ourselves and love each other in the face of all of this violence and destruction, then what have we become? What is life after all, but a gift of wondrously complex beauty?

I do not know who or where I would be without having given myself over to the creative process. I write to live. I write to co-create the future for myself and for our dreams. This is not just a survival mechanism; helping to process intense pain and betrayal, offering release, invention, recognition and transformation.

This creative act for the artist is a celebration of the infinite gifts of the Divine—the truly radiant layers of self coming into being. Poetry reveals the magical doors between waking and dreaming. Poetry reveals the hidden symbols of everything that we are. Poetry is the golden ticket home, as we awaken to the majesty and miraculous nature of Infinity. And in this way, poetry is at the peak of the magical arts. Poetry is incantation and subtle discovery of Creation.

Honestly, I was not inclined to share these intimate feelings and visions with anyone. And for a long time after even deciding to publish these poems at all, I clung to the idea of using a pseudonym. Yet somehow, for this work and all that it yearns to be, my desire for privacy seemed impossible in the face of everything that is being born. This work spoke out to me, asking me to be its guardian in the world so that it could flower forth in the gardens of our hearts. And like any aspect of life that would serve as a gift of healing, its truest expression will be in our collective actions towards creating in our reality the world we are dreaming of, and in our efforts towards a more authentic, balanced and compassionate earth community that preserves life and knowledge with integrity.

And so here we are after all this time, just you and me. I hope that you may receive these humble words in the spirit of life, the greatest gift. Please tell me your story when the time comes.

Appendix I: The Images

Blue Moon by Natalee Potter 5
Photograph. 2011

Rose's Deep Passion by Ludmila Disa 16
Photograph. 2007

Doe Ray Me Fluff by Nickole Alexandria Pepera 33
Felt Tip Pen/ San Francisco Milk Fluff/Origami Paper. 2010

The Phoenix Has Had Her Day by Nickole Alexandria Pepera 34
Gauche/Watercolor/Colored pencil. 2009

Cold Sunset by Ludmila Disa 36
Photograph. 2006

Luz' Flower by Ludmila Disa 37
Photograph. 2006

Endogénesis by Ludmila Disa 42
Photograph. 2006

Celestial Vision by Ludmila Disa 43
Photograph. 2006

Forest After the Rain by Matthieu Aubry 45
Photograph. 2009

No India in You by Nickole Alexandria Pepera 50
Inkpen/Colored pencil/ India ink. 2009

From My Lonely Tower I See by Ludmila Disa 58
Photograph. 2006

Sail on the Wings of Hope by Ludmila Disa 60
Photograph. 2006

New Zealand Redwood Forest by Matthieu Aubry 62
Photograph. 2009

Nibiru by Ludmila Disa 66
Photograph. 2006

Yes by Christina Carney 69
Mixed media. 2010

Fuerza del Sol by Ludmila Disa 70
Photograph. 2006

Colours of Peace by Ludmila Disa 79
Photograph. 2008

Bush in New Zealand by Matthieu Aubry 90
Photograph. 2009

Small by Ludmila Disa 99
Photograph. Mar de las Pampas. 2007

Burn my Rose by Ludmila Disa 102
Photograph. Mar de las Pampas. 2007

Coricancha Passage by Ludmila Disa 109
Photograph. Templo del Sol. 2007

Scenes from a Memory by Ludmila Disa 110
Photograph. Bariloche, Argentina. 2007

Appendix II: The Artists

There is a curious amount of synchronicity in the events leading to the inclusion of the dreamlike imagery that is in this book. I offer to each of these individuals my sincere and heartfelt gratitude for sharing and for entrusting me with the fruits of their craft. And for you, dearest, here is a brief vision of the artists.

Nickole Alexandria Pepera

Nickole Alexandria Pepera lives off of ice cream, swims like a porpoise and paints watercolor paintings based on her experiences with Ancient Egyptian Mescaline. She worships a cat named Stretchy and prefers wearing dresses and harassing the general public.

robotdreamer99@hotmail.com

Natalee Potter

Natalee Potter began her career in photography to capture the best possible images of her son. She is a self-taught artist, focusing most of her time on her dear family and her creative enterprise, Potterfly Photography. Future plans include establishing a natural light studio & publishing a children's book featuring her photography. If she doesn't pick up her camera at least once a day, Natalee feels like she has forgotten something—when she sees something ideal, she wants to capture it.

potterflyphotography@gmail.com
Potterflyphotography.com

Christina Carney

Christina Carney prefers to speak in the language of archetype and image and has put herself in service to the Divine Creative Source. At the time of this printing, Christina was far away from virtual techno-magic like telephones and email, and her final permission for sharing a photograph could not be found. She remains in Australia, and in the Imagination.

cmcarney07@yahoo.com.

Matthieu Aubry

Matthieu Aubry is a French photographer who has a particular interest in people. He spent 10 months living and experiencing India where it changed his perspective on life permanently. He has put together a small collection of his photographs which are his own interpretation and a preview of the spirit of India and its people. His next venture includes time in Indonesia, Cambodia and New Zealand. He will continue to document life as he sees it.

http://matthieu.net

Ludmila Disa

Ludmila Disa is an artist from Buenos Aires, Argentina. She focuses on many creative disciplines, such as graphic design, literature and music. Inspired by her parents who are painters and deeply related to Antahkarana esotericism and spirituality, she developed a personal interest in engaging many subjects simultaneously. In addition to being a natural writer, Ludmila is the vocalist of metal band Dæmon Lost, a force on the music scene in Buenos Aires. She began her love affair with photography to show the world her point of view about Nature and humankind:

"I sometimes set up scenes for shooting, but there's nothing like traveling, keeping your eyes open and the camera ready for anything that may happen or suddenly pop up into your eyes. Whether it is a little, beautiful detail of life or a huge Masterpiece of Nature, there's always a good reason for trying hard to get the picture that most resembles your point of view."

www.black-velvet-lady.deviantart.com

www.myspace.com/daemonlost

Me

I am the proud Papi of a Fairy Princess, though am not myself a Fairy King.—living in endless hours' negotiations to free the Queen of Bees from Her Highness' illusory prison beyond the icy borders of Dreamlandia. I have given up my role in the psyche wars, and am living soul for Soul, both in Mystery & here on Earth . I am in Love with a Miraculous Maiden, once the Hummingbird Ambassador of All the Stars. Since then she has left All of this Glory to come and teach us how to Dance. As in the Beginning, All is Miraculous Freedom—∞ Wine for Roses, Ballads for Milk.

When all of this is over, let me sing a song for You

Dream On

We are constantly reinforcing

Our own static assumptions about Reality

Locked into constant projections, most of which we are unconscious of,

And our projective identification—

when we take the projections of another person as being the only truth of life

It is we Sleepers who must Awaken—

awaken to the majestic, subtle and indescribable beauty of life and love

Let the Dreamers

co-create our new visions,

new worlds

Our new and infinite existence

Dream on true lovers

www.ingramcontent.com/pod-product-compliance
Lightning Source LLC
Chambersburg PA
CBHW042008150426
43195CB00002B/54